# Roger the Pronoun

Written by Coert Voorhees
Illustrations by Powerhouse Animation

# Meet the Parts of Speech

I name a specific person, place, thing, or idea. It's a big responsibility, naming things—a responsibility that requires a certain attention to detail.

Vinny the Action Verb

Some people say I'm all over the place. Some people call me a ball of energy. I take that as a compliment, because I just like to go, go, go!

I take the place of one or more Nouns or Pronouns. I always want the Noun's job, and I hang out with the Verb and Adjective.

Lucy the Linking Verb

I'm perfectly happy to link Nouns and Pronouns with the appropriate Adjectives, but it's not like I'm going to expend a lot of energy doing so.

I modify a Noun or Pronoun. I tell what kind, which one, how many, or how much. I pride myself on being the most artistic of the parts of speech.

Connie the Conjunction

Gather 'round everybody and let's have ourselves a wonderful time. I just love bringing words and groups of words together, don't you?

I modify a Verb, Adjective, or other Adverb. I tell how, when, where, to what extent, and under what condition. I often end in –ly, but I don't have to.

Izzy the Interjection

I express emotion!! Yep, I'm always here, always ready with my commas and exclamation points, just in case.

They call me Preposition because I'm pre-positioned. I'm first. At the front. Before every other word in the phrase? Got it?

Slang

I am a chameleon. A spy. An undercover operative. I infiltrate the sentence and act as whatever part of speech suits me.

ROGER THE PRONOUN




Graphic Design by Mckee Frazior
Printed by Friesens, Altona, Manitoba, Canada





This book is typeset in Komika Text

Distributed throughout the world by Ingram Publisher Services www.ingrambook.com

Printed in Canada

Roger the pronoun usually spent most of his day with Nelson.

A pronoun's job was to take the place of one or more nouns or pronouns.

Roger, please pack up that sandwich for Vinny.
I will pack it up for him .
Instead of saying the nouns again, Roger replaced them with pronouns.

If Roger wasn't paying attention, the pronoun wouldn't agree with the word it replaced, called the "antecedent."

Everyone loved Nelson, and Roger was jealous.
He felt he was destined for more.

One night, when he was feeling sad, he practiced his reflexive pronouns. He looked at himself in the mirror.
I need to give myself a pep talk.
something
It
this
whatever

Then he tried an intensive pronoun, which emphasized the word it referred to.
You're a PROnoun!
You yourself are no amateur noun.
something
It
this
whatever

The next day, Roger opened up his own shop right below Nelson's Nouns.

Nelson didn't think Roger's idea was a very good one.

Roger started by offering personal pronouns.
Want to replace the name of a person or thing? Step right up!
they
we
I
you
he
she
Subjective
them
us
me
you
him
Objective

Of course, with no antecedents, Roger's customers were confused.
It
It
It
It
It
It
It
It
It
I'd like it please.
Which it?
It. I'd like it.

Roger tried using demonstrative pronouns to distinguish the various items from one another.
This?
No.
That?
No.
Those?
No.
It
It
It
Lol.

When Vinny accidentally walked away with something, Roger had to use possessive pronouns.
That's mine.
It
It
It
It
It

In the midst of this chaos, Nelson came down to ask for a favor.
Roger, can you watch my store for a minute?
It
It
It
But because of the confusion, nobody noticed.

It's not yours, and it's not his or hers or even theirs. It's mine!
You're so possessive!
It
It
It
It
It
It

Later, Roger went upstairs to get some advice from Nelson. It didn't seem like anyone was home, so Roger had to use indefinite pronouns.

d that's when things got strange.
You're under arrest for the disappearance of Nelson the noun.
Me?

Benny took Roger downtown, where he questioned him about a possible noun/pronoun disagreement.

What more do you know?

oger professed his innocence, using
nterrogative pronouns to start questions.
Whom was I with today? What are you talking about?
We have witnesses!
Who?
Fortunately, a visitor arrived to see him.

It was Nelson, who had been searching for Roger everywhere.
Oops.
You look tired.
It gets exhausting using only nouns all the time.

: turned out that Nelson needed Roger as much as Roger
eeded Nelson. It was time for a reciprocal pronoun.
I'm so happy we found each other!

NELSON'S NOUNS
featuring
"It" by Roger

You can be my antecedent any day.

NELSON'S NOUNS
featuring "It" by Roge
keys/ those
tie/his
cake/that
ball/theirs
purse/hers
jellyfish/ something

Pronouns:
You, me, this, and
that over there

# PRONOUNS

**A pronoun takes the place of one or more nouns or pronouns.**

## REPLACING NOUNS

Frederick spilled a jar of mayonnaise on my mother and father.

He spilled it on them.

# REPLACING PRONOUNS:

He and she came to my house yesterday.

They came to my house yesterday.

## SUBJECTIVE PERSONAL PRONOUNS

A subjective personal pronoun acts as the subject of the sentence.

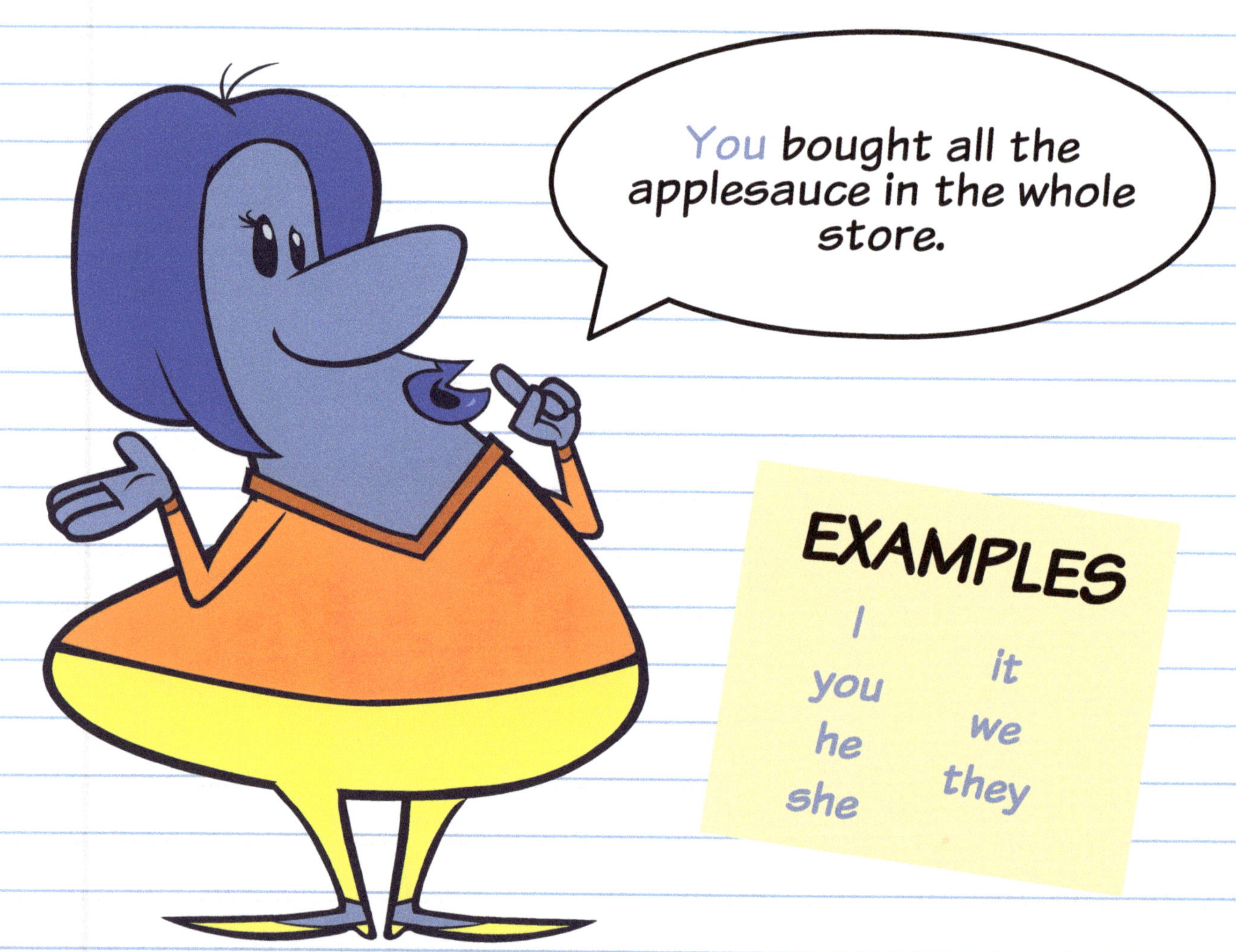


**EXAMPLES**

I
you
he
she
it
we
they

## OBJECTIVE PERSONAL PRONOUNS

An objective personal pronoun acts as the object of a verb, preposition, or infinitive phrase.

**EXAMPLES:** me, you, her, him, it, us, them

**Reggie threw me a bag of nachos.**

Indirect object of the verb threw.

**Vinny and Lucy invited us to the play!**

Direct object of the verb invited.

**Izzy did their homework for them.**

Object of the preposition for.

**The piano was so out of tune that Jake begged Doctor Noize not to play it.**

Object of the infinitive phrase to play

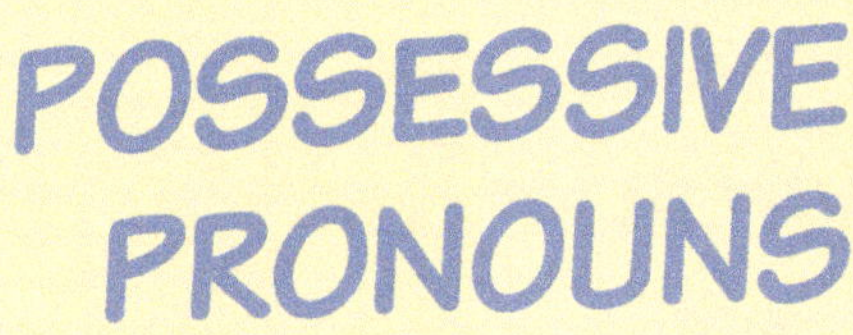


A possessive pronoun shows ownership or possession.

The computer is ours.

Sometimes Patricia likes to take things that are mine and not hers.

**EXAMPLES**

| | |
|---|---|
| mine | yours |
| his | hers |
| ours | theirs |

# INTERROGATIVE PRONOUNS

An interrogative pronoun is used to ask a question. Usually the antecedent is unknown, which is the reason for the question.

## EXAMPLES

what who
whom which
whose

A demonstrative pronoun replaces one or more nouns and indicates proximity (near or far).

This is Pete's science project.

Those are my shoes.

**EXAMPLES**

this that
these those

# INDEFINITE PRONOUNS

An indefinite pronoun does not refer to a specific noun or pronoun. Often, the antecedent is unknown.

## EXAMPLES

everyone
anybody
another

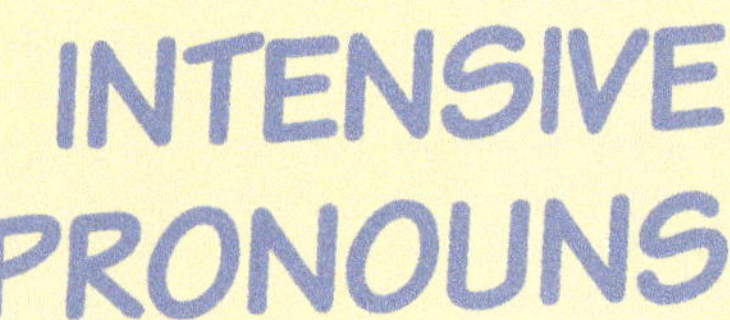

# INTENSIVE PRONOUNS

An intensive pronoun emphasizes, or intensifies, a noun or another pronoun.

You yourself are the biggest goofball in the world.

Yes, I baked all those cookies myself.

## EXAMPLES

myself
yourself
himself
herself
itself
ourselves
yourselves
themselves

# REFLEXIVE PRONOUNS

A refelexive pronoun directs the action of the verb back to the subject of the sentence.

## RELATIVE PRONOUNS

A relative pronoun introduces an adjective clause, which is a subordinate clause that modifies one or more nouns or pronouns.

My mother, who is a biologist, loves to scuba dive.

Gerladine prefers chocolate that tastes like raspberries.

### EXAMPLES

that which
who whom
whose

CPSIA information can be obtained
at www.ICGtesting.com
Printed in the USA
BVHW050527110519
547997BV00001B/1/P